Robert Pattinson
Eternally Yours

To Colleen AF Venable, who inspires

The author would like to thank Martha Mihalick and
Molly O'Neill for their invaluable contributions to this project.

Insert: pages 1, 2, 3 (top), 5, 8, © The Barnes Theatre Company; pages 3 (middle),
4 (top), © JIL Studio/Getty Images; page 4 (bottom), © Fred Duval/Getty Images;
pages 3 (bottom), 6, 7, © Amy Howe Photography.

Library of Congress Cataloging-in-Publication Data is available.
ISBN 978-0-06-176553-7

Typography by Pamela Darcy of Neo9 Design, Inc.
❖
First Edition

Robert Pattinson

Eternally Yours

An Unauthorized Biography

By Isabelle Adams

HarperEntertainment

An Imprint of HarperCollinsPublishers

Contents

Introduction
Be Still Our Hearts!

Robert Pattinson never expected to be haunting the dreams of millions of teenage girls around the world. In fact, the thousands of screaming fans usually make him blush! But this gifted (and stunningly attractive) young actor better get used to the attention because his starring role as the world's hottest vampire has secured his spot in our hearts.

In just two breakout roles, Robert Pattinson has gone from being a minor hottie to an all-out, major heartthrob. And he's gone from extreme to extreme as far as the roles he's played. In the movie adaptation of J. K. Rowling's *Harry Potter and the Goblet of Fire*, the life of his character—doomed, handsome athlete, schoolboy, and all-around good guy, Cedric Diggory— was tragically cut short. Then, as dazzling Edward Cullen in the movie version of Stephenie Meyer's *Twilight*, he played another schoolboy, but this time one who can *never* die, and is eternally frozen at the age of seventeen, denying his dark nature for the sake of true love. What's the link? Both characters are exceedingly noble and outrageously crush worthy!

It's not just the characters that have something in common, either. *Twilight* also happens to be the most popular young-adult book since the Harry Potter series. So Robert Pattinson certainly owes a big thank-you to fans of both bestselling book series, since without the readers who love them, he might still be an unknown.

Not long before *Harry Potter and the Goblet of*

Fire was released, an interviewer met with Robert. At that time Triwizard champion Cedric was his biggest role to date. In between talking about his fellow actors and his band, Robert was asked what his next project would be. After all, what could possibly follow a global phenomenon like *Harry Potter*?

Robert tossed out several possibilities. He'd gotten his acting start in live theater productions, so he was considering returning to that. He also wanted to do something "weird." There had recently been a part he'd *really* wanted. The choice came down to him and one other guy—but the other guy got it. (Bet those casting directors are kicking themselves now!) Oh, and there was an American movie that he'd been offered, one that would involve him signing on for the possibility of at least three movies. . . .

At the time, fans had no idea that he was referring to *Twilight* and the successive possible movie sequels based on bestselling author Stephenie Meyer's Twilight

Saga. It's almost guaranteed that Robert had no idea how many fans the *Twilight* movie would have. But we're certainly glad that he said yes to that offer!

So how did a shy guy from a quiet London suburb end up as part of not one but two worldwide phenomena by the age of twenty-two? He has beautiful eyes and chiseled cheekbones, it's true, but he's also charming and talented—and he's a musician to boot! There's no doubt that Robert Pattinson is here to stay, and that's something to cheer about!

Rob's Dazzling Roots

"Twelve was a turning point, as I moved to a mixed school, and then I became cool and discovered hair gel."
—*Robert Pattinson*

Robert Thomas-Pattinson was born on May 13, 1986, in Barnes, a suburb of London, the capital of England. London has been a major settlement for over two thousand years, and is one of the world's leading centers for business, finance, and culture. It has a widely diverse population—more than three hundred languages are spoken in London. Robert grew up in an affluent and rather secluded area near the Thames

River, full of rich culture and elegant houses. And yes, we can thank his London upbringing for that a-maz-ing-ly sexy accent!

Lucky for Robert, two of his passions—music and theater—are significant influences in Barnes. The recording studio Olympic Studios, one of the town's prominent attractions, has hosted some of the biggest stars of pop and rock music, from the Beatles to Madonna to Coldplay. Another tourist site is the Old Sorting Office Arts Centre, which has become a key name in art and fringe theater. The Old Sorting Office hosts both art exhibits and theater productions, all open to the public. A teenage Robert played key roles in the Old Sorting Office's stage productions. After spending his early years in an area so supportive of the arts, it's no surprise that Robert has quickly risen to such heights in his acting career.

Robert is the youngest of three kids in the Pattinson family, and the only son. He has two older sisters. Elizabeth is three years older than he is, and Victoria is five years older. Robert's father, Richard, is a second-hand car dealer who specializes in importing vintage cars from America, and when Rob was growing up, his mother, Clare, worked for a modeling agency. Perhaps she's even the one who encouraged Rob to pursue the modeling he's done at various parts of his career.

Robert's dad loves that his son is involved in a creative profession. According to Robert: "My dad said to me the other day, 'I really am an artistic person.' I was shocked as I never saw him as creative. I think me and my sisters are living out that side of him as my sister is another creative person. She's a songwriter." Robert's sister Elizabeth, better known as Lizzy, has established herself in the music industry in England. Lizzy is both a singer and a songwriter. A scout from EMI, one of the "big four" major record labels, discovered her when she was seventeen. It seems that the Pattinson family's creative talents spring up strongly in their teenage years, because Robert, too, got his big break at age seventeen. In the

United Kingdom, Lizzy is the songwriting brains—
and often the onstage talent—behind a number of
bands that are known for hitting the top of the charts
with catchy pop tunes.

Lizzy has performed with the band Aurora UK,
which is a trio based in London. Lizzy's bandmates
are the keyboardist Simon Greenaway and guitarist
Sacha Collisson; Lizzy is the singer of the group. The
dance band's debut single was "Dreaming," and their
first album, released in 2002, was titled the same. In
fact, Lizzy can fill in her younger brother on the peaks
and pitfalls of skyrocketing fame, because by the time
she was eighteen, Aurora UK had had not one but
two Top Twenty hits: "Dreaming" and "The Day It
Rained Forever."

Aurora UK toured throughout the United Kingdom, North America, and Europe. They played in
many major music venues, and the concert crowds
often numbered more than 100,000 screaming fans!
Lizzy recently collaborated with Aurora UK again on

a 2006 song called "Summer Son." Aurora UK isn't the only band Lizzy Pattinson sings for, though. She's also worked with Milk & Sugar, singing "Let the Sunshine In," which hit the number one spot on the Billboard Dance Chart.

Robert and Lizzy's middle sister, Victoria, isn't involved in the music or theater world, but she channels the Pattinson creativity in another way, putting it to good use in her job in advertising. Unfortunately for Robert, his sisters' creativity wasn't always beneficial to him. "Up until I was twelve my sisters used to dress me up as a girl and introduce me as 'Claudia,'" he says. Growing up with two sisters might have had its pitfalls, but chances are it means Rob learned how to treat girls right early on. And anyway, "Twelve was a turning point, as I moved to a mixed school [a school with boys and girls], and then I became cool and discovered hair gel." Apparently trademark hair has been a part of Robert's persona ever since. At a press event promoting *Twilight*, a *Washington Post* reporter quizzed Robert on how he gets his artfully messy hair to stick up so perfectly. Robert laughed and said, "You just don't wash it. Ever."

Back to Robert's life history and the days in which he was first discovering hair gel . . . along with first discovering his talent for acting. The first school Robert attended was an all-boys school called the Tower House School. Tower House is located in a suburb close to Barnes, an area known for schools with high standards for excellence. Traditionally, a "tower house" could also be called a castle—a building built for either defense or for living in. The Tower House School is a preparatory school for boys ages four to thirteen. Music, art, and drama are considered a vital part of the Tower House School curriculum, and Robert got his first taste of acting while he was a student there. He began performing in school productions at age six. His roles included the King of Hearts (aww!) in a play written by one of the teachers called *Spell for a Rhyme* and Robert in William

Golding's *Lord of the Flies.*

"He wasn't a particularly academic child but he always loved drama," said Caroline Booth, a school secretary, to the *Evening Standard.* "He was an absolutely lovely boy, everyone adored him. We have lots of lovely boys here but he was something special. He was very pretty, beautiful and blond." Even back then, people appreciated Rob's talents—and his undeniable cuteness. Caroline Booth continued, "I wouldn't say he was a star but he was very keen on our drama club. We're all so pleased that he's found something he really shines at."

How else could his teachers and classmates tell that Robert was more interested in the theater than academics? Well, in a newsletter during his last year there, he was called "a runaway winner of last term's Form Three untidy desk award." Robert did serve as a lunch monitor at his school, but he wasn't always the best monitor, either. "I used to take everyone's chips!" he told the BBC. Not that this mischievous French fry thief wasn't ever the victim of pranks himself. "Someone stole my shoelaces once from my shoes," a younger Rob once revealed. "I still wear them and never put laces in them—they're like my trademark shoes now!" And even Robert acknowledges that he didn't have the best school reports. "They were always pretty bad—I never ever did my homework. I always turned up for lessons, as I liked my teachers, but my report said I didn't try very hard."

No question, Robert must have been a bit of a scoundrel, since he also admitted that he was expelled from school when he was twelve, though he wouldn't confess what, exactly, had caused that bit of drama! But his expulsion led to a change that Rob probably didn't mind all too much, after spending years with only other boys for classmates. The switch in schools meant that he started attending a co-ed school. And it seems he wasted no time getting to know some of those girls quite well, because he told *Seventeen* magazine that he had his first kiss at age twelve, too!

The Harrodian School was good for more than Rob's budding love life. It was a superb environment for a creative teenager. The school takes students—boys *and* girls—from ages four to eighteen and encourages them to reach their full potential, academically, physically, and socially. They also want their students to become well-rounded people who contribute positive things to the world. The curriculum at Harrodian encourages manners, consideration, and awareness of society and the world. It's not a large school, as the student body has fewer than one thousand students. But students there have lots of privileges. They have a heated outdoor swimming pool on the grounds for use in the summer and autumn terms, as well as science laboratories, a state-of-the-art computer lab, and a music and dramatic studies center.

American students might get a bit of culture shock if they attended the Harrodian School. The school's rules are certainly more strict than those we're used to here in the United States. Students there are expected to "line up quietly outside the classroom until told to enter by the teacher" and are not to have "graffiti" on their schoolbook covers. Leaving the school premises without permission can even result in "immediate expulsion"! And there's a very preppy dress code. While Robert attended the Harrodian School, he had to wear either gray or black trousers, a collared shirt and navy sweater, and dark socks and shoes. He wasn't allowed to wear hooded tops, sweaters with logos besides the school's, blue jeans or jean jackets, T-shirts under shirts, or athletic shoes. Boys aren't permitted to wear jewelry of any sort at Harrodian, and their haircuts can't be "extreme in style or length." (It's a good thing hair gel was still allowed.) On the plus side, though, all that emphasis on decorum creates a great reputation for the school. According to the school's website, "First-rate drama productions, art exhibitions, and musical events are features of Harrodian life, and a wide range of extracurricular activities is offered each term."

Students at the Harrodian School are divided into four houses—just like at Hogwarts! The houses are named Bridge, Ferry, Lonsdale, and Thames, and each student is allocated a house when they enter the school. According to Harrodian's website: "Students are able to gain house points through Sport, Drama, Music, Public Speaking, Debating, and Citizenship." There's even the equivalent of the House Cup, though it has a slightly different name! Whichever house has the most points at the end of each term is presented with the Gallagher Shield. And, like Hogwarts, the school names a Head Boy and Head Girl each year, thought Robert never held that coveted title as his character Cedric did. Asked by the BBC who his favorite, most memorable teacher was, Robert replied, "Probably my English teacher because she got me into writing instead of just answering the question. I used to hand in homework with twenty pages of nonsense and she'd still mark it. She was a really amazing teacher." Robert has already proved two major creative talents—acting and music—perhaps someday we'll see his success as a writer, too.

Robert's teenage life wasn't all school, though. He was an active athlete, skiing, snowboarding, and playing soccer. He had a job, too. "I started doing a paper round when I was about ten," he said. "I started earning ten pounds [around twenty American dollars] a week and then I was obsessed with earning money until I was about fifteen." These days Robert has a much more sensible view of money. In an interview with music website virginmedia.com, he said he didn't want to look for a recording contract for his music until he felt absolutely ready. "My sister works so hard to make money and I think it ruins you," he concluded. Robert's business sense got him through the end of school, though, so it's good he has a level head for money matters. After he got his first screen acting job, he needed the income to pay for school. He told a London newspaper, the *Evening Standard*, "At the time, my father said to me, 'Okay, you might as well leave school now, since you're not working very hard.' And when I told him I wanted to stay on for my A levels, he said I'd have to pay my own fees—then he'd pay me back if I got good enough grades."

Wait! Is school optional in England?! Well, not completely, no. But the final two years of high school *are* optional. Students who complete those two years have to take Advanced levels (A levels)—a kind of super-intensive final exam. Many English universities consider the A levels an entrance examination—like the SATs or ACTs—requiring students to achieve a certain grade in order to be admitted. Often, A level classes—especially at small schools like Harrodian School—can be tiny. Robert's year had only six students! Unfortunately he didn't make good enough grades for his dad to pay him back. Remember that untidy desk award? Even though Robert wanted to complete his final two years, he quickly realized that he much preferred working in the theater to school. And since the same casting agent who helped him get that first screen part also helped him land the role of Cedric Diggory, Robert's focus on acting over academics paid off in the end.

We have Robert's dad to thank for his entrance into the acting world, though, so don't be too hard on him for not paying for those last two years of school. When asked how he became serious about acting, Robert responds, "My dad saw a bunch of pretty girls in a restaurant and he asked them where they came from and they said drama group. He said, 'Son, that is where you need to go.'" And it seems that suggestion was all the convincing that Robert needed. He was off to join the world of professional theater!

A Superstar Career Begins

"**Sometimes I realize I could be working at a shoe shop. Acting is much cooler.**" —*Robert Pattinson*

At age fifteen, Robert joined the Barnes Theatre Company, a local performance group that produced two shows each year. This is certainly a case of Robert being in the right place at the right time; the Barnes Theatre Company is located just around the corner from the house he grew up in. Okay, maybe he *did* join thinking about the cute girls he might meet, at his dad's suggestion, but—potential girlfriends aside—he knew acting was something he enjoyed, and something that he had the potential to be quite good at. Robert told Scholastic, the American publisher of the Harry Potter books, "I really wasn't part of the acting fraternity at my school, but I joined this thing after my dad argued with me for ages. I think he had some sort of weird foresight about it." Sometimes it really does pay to listen to the parents—even when they're annoying.

Robert didn't leap right into acting lead roles, though. First he put in some time doing work backstage, which he admits was good for his somewhat oversize teenage ego. "I wasn't nervous of performing," he told *StageCoach Magazine*, "but at sixteen, I thought it would be arrogant [to admit that]!" In a local theater group, backstage work like Robert did could have included anything from helping to build and paint sets, to helping with costumes or changing furniture between scenes. Often, the backstage helpers are called techies because some create and run the technical aspects like lighting and sound. Most techies wear all black so that they are harder to see in the wings while a play is being performed. There's no way a hottie like Robert was going to blend into the crowd, though, and as he says, "For some reason when I finished the backstage thing, I just decided that I should try to act. So I auditioned for *Guys and Dolls*."

Guys and Dolls is a musical that was first produced in 1950, but has found lasting popularity as a choice for high schools and community theaters. It's about two high-stakes gamblers and the ladies they're in love with. The lead role is Nathan Detroit, a guy who's trying to find a new location for his illegal card-playing game. He makes a bet that another high-rolling gambler, Sky Masterson, can't get Sarah, the straitlaced lady in charge of the local missionary organization, to agree to a dinner date—in Havana, Cuba. With the typical crossed signals, mixed messages, laughter, and happy ending of a musical, Nathan and his on-again, off-again girlfriend, Adelaide, and the new couple, Sky and Sarah, fight, cry, make amends, and in the end profess their true love. *Guys and Dolls* received a Tony Award the first year it was on Broadway, and has been revived on Broadway, in the West End (London's version of Broadway), and in Australia. Robert, of course, was gunning for the lead, the role of Nathan Detroit, the same role that Frank Sinatra played in the movie version of *Guys and Dolls*. Disappointingly, though, he "got an embarrassing Cuban dancer part." Still, Robert showed his dedication to the company and to acting in general by giving the bit part his all. That paid off, because as Robert told *StageCoach*, "They respected me for doing it and gave me the lead in Thornton Wilder's *Our Town*—and that got me an agent."

It may be rather odd to think of *Our Town*, the quintessential American play, being produced in a small theater in England. But this may have been the first time Robert got to practice his American accent! *Our Town* is an older play than *Guys and Dolls*. It was first performed in 1938, and the American playwright Thornton Wilder won a Pulitzer Prize for writing it. *Our Town* tells the story of a small New England town called Grover's Corners, and of Emily Webb and George Gibbs, who fall in love as teenagers. The play is in three acts: the first showing a typical day in town, with Emily agreeing to help George with his homework; the second showing Emily and George's wedding day; and the third showing a sadder day— the day of Emily's funeral. Although the play has its sad moments, its main theme is to remind theater-goers to appreciate every second of even the most ordinary days. Robert played the lead role of George Gibbs, who has the strongest and most difficult emo- tional arc, and even as a teenager, Rob was surely up to that task.

Robert also starred in the Barnes Theatre Company's production of *Anything Goes*, a musical, also from the 1930s. *Anything Goes* is one of the famous musicals with music and lyrics by Cole Porter, and it debuted on

Broadway in 1934. It's been revived numerous times in both the United States and in the United Kingdom. There are two movie versions of it as well! Set on an ocean liner, with stowaways, star-crossed lovers, nightclub singers, public enemies, wealthy aristocrats, and heiresses, it's a story full of madcap antics. Robert played the role of Lord Evelyn Oakleigh, a stuffy and unlucky Englishman who ends up losing one fiancée and winning another. Come to think of it, after that first small dancing part in *Guys and Dolls*, in his key roles both onstage and on-screen, Rob has portrayed good-hearted guys seeking true love. It's no wonder we think he's the perfect guy!

Robert has nothing but positive things to say about his experience with the Barnes Theatre Company. He told scholastic.com, "They used to do two shows a year and they are all great. So many people from there had become actors. The directors were actors themselves and were very talented." He added, "I owe everything to that little club." We imagine that he's made his old directors quite proud of their former student, too!

The Barnes Theatre Company isn't the only local theater in his area of London, and Robert also found acting work from his mid-to-late teens with the Old Sorting Office Arts Centre. The Centre is a vital part of Barnes's social and cultural life. According to the Old Sorting Office's website, the OSO Arts Centre "provides a venue for theatre and live performances, art exhibitions, dance classes, music, drama for all ages and abilities, writers' groups, a film club, yoga, Pilates classes, education opportunities . . . in fact, anything and everything." The stage manager who worked at OSO throughout Robert's years there remembers him well as a "smashing kid." She confirms what Robert now freely admits, saying, "I think he only joined because of the girls!" She went on to mention that Rob still goes back to visit his old OSO friends when he's in England and "is always welcome." And she says that it's been rewarding to follow Robert's career since he left the OSO, remarking, "It's quite lovely to see that he's gone on to do so well." Sounds like everyone who knew Robert in his younger years is delighted to know about the success that this budding star is finding.

At the Old Sorting Office, Robert won the role of Malcolm in Shakespeare's stage classic *Macbeth*. This is a tragic play: Macbeth, an honored soldier in Scotland, grows so power hungry that he and his wife conspire to murder the king in order to place Macbeth on the throne. Malcolm is the true king's son, who flees Macbeth's greed, but eventually returns to take the throne and reestablish order in the kingdom. In other words, this, too, was a fitting, noble role for the young man who has now become a symbol of nobility because of his role as a "vegetarian" vampire.

But though it's nice to get the girl and be the noble hero most of the time, Robert likes playing the bad guy every now and then, too! The first time he did this was also his first true period role—as Alec in the

OSO's production of *Tess of the D'Urbervilles.* The play is based on a Victorian novel by Thomas Hardy, published in 1891. *Tess* is a tragic drama about a young peasant woman whose family tries to force her to marry someone well-off to bring them better circumstances. Alec, the young man whom Robert played, is an unsavory character—a big difference from those three previous roles. While he probably didn't get to twirl a villainous mustache or perfect a dastardly laugh, this role gave him his first experience in playing a death scene, something he could call on for his later role as doomed Cedric Diggory in *Harry Potter.*

From the live stage to the big screen wasn't too giant a leap for Robert. It was clear to anyone who saw him perform that he'd been bitten by the acting bug, and that he might just have what it takes to make it on-screen. Robert's first film role was in a German made-for-television movie called *Ring of the Nibelungs,* which aired in 2004. The story is based on the Germanic and Nordic legends that inspired J. R. R. Tolkien's *Lord of the Rings,* as well as the composer Richard Wagner's famed Ring Cycle operas. In *Ring of the Nibelungs,* a young blacksmith named Siegfried, who doesn't know he's actually heir to a kingdom, slays a dragon and accepts a cursed hoard of gold as his reward.

Robert was just seventeen at the time that he played a small part as Giselher, a king's son. *Ring of the Nibelungs* filmed in Cape Town, South Africa. Robert told virginmedia.com, "I was there for three months in an apartment at just seventeen! So I came back really confident." *Ring of the Nibelungs* is called *Dark Kingdom: The Dragon King* here in the United States. The movie was Robert's first time with filming special effects, which, he said, "are probably one of the strangest things to go into if you have never done acting before." It's a good thing that he got experience working with special effects on this smaller scale, because he would soon have much more intense special effects to act with in *Harry Potter* and *Twilight.* After all, it's not in every film that an actor plays a part that involves running across treetops and making his skin sparkle like diamonds!

The year 2004 was a busy one for Rob. Besides the role in *Ring of the Nibelungs*, he also filmed a small part in the major film *Vanity Fair*, which starred Reese Witherspoon as a social-climbing antiheroine named Becky Sharp. Another Victorian period piece, *Vanity Fair* is an adaptation of the 1847 novel by William Makepeace Thackeray. Robert's role was Becky's grown son, Rawdy Crawley. Sadly for Robert's fans seeking that footage, his scenes were cut from the theatrical version of the film—but some are available in the DVD extras.

Robert's best friend, Tom Sturridge, also had a small part in *Vanity Fair*. Tom and Robert had met through Tom's siblings, who attended the Harrodian School with Robert. The two guys have been friends for years and are often photographed out on the town together, enjoying each other's company, comparing notes on movie work, and likely reminiscing about all the trouble they got into together during their shared school days.

Besides acting, Robert did some modeling work in his late teens and early twenties as well—no surprise there, given his dashing good looks and killer smile (not to mention that über-sexy, just-rolled-out-of-bed hair)! He modeled at times under the more formal name of Robert Thomas-Pattinson, perhaps to distinguish the modeling from his rapidly growing acting résumé. His most widely seen campaign was for the British clothing label Hackett. Robert, along with fellow heartthrobs Matthew Goode and Jamie Strachan, was selected for Hackett's Autumn/Winter 2007 line, and wise choices they all were. Hackett, according to its website, "is a classic British clothing and accessories brand which caters for the head to toe needs of men of all ages who wish to dress stylishly and to whom quality is more important than the vagaries of fashion." In other words, Hackett aims to represent the tradition of British clothing without being old-fashioned.

A peek at the Hackett website (or a search online for Rob's shots from the advertising campaign) reveals just the sort of impeccably groomed, timeless attire that pops to mind with the words, "British gentleman." And with classically good-looking men like Robert Pattinson wearing the clothes, how can they look anything but dashing? Robert talks very little about his modeling stints, but that's why they say a picture is worth a thousand words!

Has Robert ever wondered what he might have been doing in those years between school and his casting as Cedric Diggory if he hadn't listened to his dad and tried acting? Scholastic asked just that question in an interview, and Robert responded, "I have no idea. I was thinking about that. I would have just gone to university and would have kind of just done the average thing." If Robert had chosen to do the "average thing," he would have applied to a university after completing his A levels in high school. Students in England get to choose which subjects they'd like to study for the A levels, and often that's what they go on to concentrate on in the university. Most British students earn their bachelor's degree in only three years, and tuitions for many schools are government funded to keep costs low for the students. Even still, Rob has his days where he feels less than confident, or when the pressures of his career get overwhelming. "Sometimes I think, 'To hell with acting.'" Luckily for all his fans, he usually snaps out of those funks pretty quickly. "And then I realize I could be working at a shoe shop. Acting is much cooler."

Rob is quick to recognize his incredible good fortune. "I was just talking to my agent about that the other day," Robert continued. "It is unbelievable that this stroke of luck has completely changed my entire life. I can't even remember what I was thinking those two years ago. Now I sort of do things differently, and I am reading all these scripts. I was out in LA a couple of weeks ago. I got an agent in LA, and it is ridiculous." But it's not so ridiculous to anyone who's seen Robert's talented performances. So it looks like fans can add "humble" to the long list of admirable traits that make him dreamy!

Breakthrough!
Rob's Champion Role

"Everyone semi-idolizes Cedric. All the girls fancy him, and the guys want to be him." —*Robert Pattinson*

The leading roles with the Barnes Theatre Company and the Old Sorting Office Arts Centre were great parts for Robert to cut his teeth on. They led to finding his agent and landing the small parts in the television movies and in *Vanity Fair*. But in 2003 came the critical moment in Robert's career: the audition for *Harry Potter and the Goblet of Fire*.

Pretty much anyone who hasn't been living under

a rock for the last ten years knows about *Harry Potter.* The Harry Potter franchise is one of the largest book and movie franchises in the world. It all began in 1998 with the book *Harry Potter and the Sorcerer's Stone* by J. K. Rowling, and the seventh and final book of the series, *Harry Potter and the Deathly Hallows*, was published in 2007. As of June 2008, the series had sold more than 400 million copies worldwide. It has been translated into sixty-seven languages—including "dead" languages like Latin! The world had never seen a far-reaching publishing phenomenon quite like Harry Potter. Fans span all ages, from elementary school kids to teenagers, to parents, and even grandparents. The last three books in the series were released with great fanfare at midnight parties around the globe. Now each book of the series, except for the final one, has been made into a blockbuster movie, full of special effects and amazing actors—including the one and only Robert Pattinson, of course.

In 2003, when Robert was seventeen, the long-awaited fifth book, *Harry Potter and the Order of the Phoenix*, had finally been published, and movies of the first two books, *Harry Potter and the Sorcerer's Stone* and *Harry Potter and the Chamber of Secrets*, had become smash hits. The third movie was in production, and the movie executives were already looking ahead to the fourth, *Harry Potter and the Goblet of Fire*. The same casting agent who suggested Robert for *Vanity Fair* suggested him for *Goblet of Fire*.

As it turns out, Rob may have been among the very few people who had still not read a single Harry Potter book, and he quickly read *Goblet of Fire* before auditioning. ("I've read three and five now as well, and I'm halfway through six!" he claims.) The day before Robert was to leave for South Africa to film *Ring of the Nibelungs*, the casting agent introduced him to Mike Newell, the director of *Goblet of Fire*. "I was the first person to be seen for any part on the film, which could have helped," Robert said. But that doesn't mean he was confident he'd gotten the part at the time! "I am now determined to do really weird parts," he continued, "but I think I overdo it in auditions so nobody really trusts me!".

Robert took off for Cape Town, South Africa, and spent three months filming *Ring of the Nibelungs*. The day he came back from that adventure, he had his callback for *Goblet of Fire* and embarked on an adventure even more remarkable. He met again with Mike Newell, who told him after the audition that he'd earned the role of Triwizard Champion Cedric Diggory. As he said to Virgin Media just before *Goblet of Fire* hit theaters, "Since I started acting it's kind of been a bit mad. I never really did anything before and two years ago I started acting and I've kind of been in work ever since. Then *Harry Potter* came along and it's been a huge step and a massive event in my life." But even Robert couldn't have possibly imagined the charmed acting life that the role of Cedric Diggory would open for him.

The plot of *Harry Potter and the Goblet of Fire*

hinges on the Triwizard Tournament, an international competition that takes place at Hogwarts School of Witchcraft and Wizardry. Two other wizard schools, Beauxbatons and Durmstrang, send their students to Hogwarts, and a champion is chosen from each to compete in three challenges throughout the academic year. Cedric Diggory is the official Hogwarts Champion—the home team favorite, if you will. Cedric is seventeen years old (the same age as Robert was during filming) and in his final year at Hogwarts. He is a part of the Hufflepuff house and, like all Hufflepuffs, is known for his dedication and hard work. But he's not just any Hufflepuff—Cedric is Head Boy, the designated representative and leader of his entire class. He is also a Quidditch player, and is one of the only Quidditch Seekers to have bested Harry during a Quidditch match.

When Robert was asked what his first impressions of the character of Cedric were, he responded, "I think he's a pretty cool character." It would be practically impossible not to like a guy like Cedric! Robert added insight to his breakout role, though, explaining, "He's not really a complete cliché of the good kid in school. He's just quiet. He is actually just a genuinely good person, but he doesn't make a big deal about it or anything. I can kind of relate to that. He's not an unattractive character at all and his story line is a nice story line to play." Discovering the nuances and different sides of a character is part of the challenge of acting, and Robert rose to the task here, finding more depth to Cedric than just being an all-around nice guy.

Cedric wants to win the Triwizard Cup and to beat Harry, who was added to the tournament as a fourth champion (and second representative of Hogwarts) through a series of peculiar events. But despite his ambition, Cedric never fights dirty. "It's impossible to hate Cedric. He's competitive but he's also a nice guy," says Robert. "Everyone semi-idolizes him. All the girls fancy him, and the guys want to be him." That's quite a tall order. Was Robert a perfect fit for such an upstanding young gentleman? According to director Mike Newell, he definitely was! "Cedric exemplifies all that you would expect the Hogwarts champion to be," Newell told the *Evening Standard*. "Robert Pattinson was born to play the role; he's quintessentially English with chiselled public schoolboy good looks."

But does Robert himself think that he's just like Cedric? It may be hard to believe, but no, he doesn't. "Not at all," he told the *Evening Standard*. "I was never a leader, and the idea of my ever being made head boy would have been a complete joke. I wasn't involved in much at school, and I was never picked for any of the teams." Playing a character he sees as quite different from himself gave Robert some new perspectives. He said during a Japanese interview, "Cedric is a really polite guy, and I wasn't really before. I became a lot more polite during the filming and I started holding open doors for people and things. And saying thank you for everything. People would say hello to me, and I would say thank you back." Holding doors open, being über-polite—*oooh la la!* If it's possible, playing the heroic Cedric Diggory made Robert even more attractive, so for that we say, "Thank you, J. K. Rowling!"

Playing Cedric was Robert's largest role to that point, but he didn't let it go to his seventeen-year-old head. Being in *Goblet of Fire* meant acting alongside some of the greatest adult actors working in Britain today, from Ralph Fiennes to Michael Gambon to Maggie Smith and more. It must have been daunting for many of the new cast members to consider. When asked if he found himself at all starstruck during his work on the movie, Robert replied, "Yeah, I did. I'm a big fan of Michael Gambon. They were all really, really nice people and they treat it as a job. They don't really have big egos or anything about it. There was one guy—Warwick Davis—he's in *Willow,* and *Willow* is like my favorite film." Can you imagine working with someone who starred in your favorite film? Robert was speechless at the experience. "I had one scene sitting next to [Warwick Davis] at the dragon task, and I had no idea what to say to him at all!" he said. "He was the only person I asked for an autograph the whole way through it!"

Being in the presence of so many experienced, renowned actors pushed Robert to do his absolute best. "I really wanted to do it really well because I'm still young and a relatively inexperienced actor," he explained quite earnestly. He funneled his nervousness into his preparation for the part, rather than sitting around fretting about it. As he told one interviewer, "I put quite a lot of work into it in the beginning. So I ignored all my nerves by sitting and looking at the script or reading the book ten times." Reading a 752-page book ten times over? Anyone would say that kind of dedication *more* than makes up for his having only read the book once before the audition!

Preparing to play Cedric Diggory wasn't just a matter of finding all of Cedric's layers or knowing the book backward and forward. Robert also had to face catapulting into the public eye as an immediate heart-throb. Not only did Robert have to do his best acting work to keep up with the legends he was working with, but he had to deal with the pressure of always looking perfect—never getting a zit or having a bad hair day (not that we actually believe that Rob could *ever* have one of those). Asked how he felt about playing such a dreamy guy, Robert answered, "That is quite difficult. In the book and also my first intro-duction of the script is like 'an absurdly handsome seventeen-year-old' and it kind of puts you off a little bit, when you're trying to act, and you're trying to get good angles to look good-looking and stuff. It's really stupid; you'd think I'm really egotistical. But I think that's the most daunting part about it—it's much scar-ier than meeting Voldemort!" Still, he wasn't entirely comfortable with one label as he gained notice for *Harry Potter and the Goblet of Fire*. "I read the *Variety* review and their only comment was 'rangy,'" he said. "I thought it meant from the range, like a cowboy.

But it just means tall and lanky." Now, modesty is an endearing quality, but we think that comment was just a moment of absurdity for Robert-slash-Cedric. Because who could ever think a hottie like Robert Pattinson is *just* tall?

Magic

"I wanted to be taken really seriously as an actor so I used to just sit around just drinking coffee all day and trying to look really intense." —*Robert Pattinson*

So what were Robert's days on the *Goblet of Fire* set like? As a new cast member joining an already tight-knit team of actors, there were sure to be some adjustments and challenges for all the actors involved. After all, the main actors had worked together on the previous Harry Potter movies and had a deep understanding of one another's working styles, as well as their personalities on and off the set. The new actors were totally outside that loop. Luckily Robert bonded quickly with two of the other new actors, whom he still counts among his close friends today—Katie Leung, who played Cedric's girlfriend, Cho Chang, and Stanislav Ianevski, who played fellow Triwizard competitor Viktor Krum. In fact, there's a hilarious clip of Robert enthusiastically hugging—er, *male bonding with*—his new pal Stan on their shared first day on set. (Just search YouTube for "Robert Pattinson hugs Krum," or look for it on the DVD extras . . . and get ready to say "awww!")

The instant camaraderie between the new actors was a fantastic bonus, but the movie's makers already had plans in place to ensure that Rob and his fellow newbies—like the other Triwizard champions—would fit right into the Harry Potter family. The shoot, which would last nearly a year, began on March 21, 2004, but Mike Newell, the movie's director, decided to have the young members of his cast meet before that. "We had two weeks of acting classes, and the reason that we did this was that I was very anxious that the established characters would not dominate the newcomers, many of whom had never acted before," Newell said in a *Goblet of Fire* press conference. "What we did was we played. We did physical exercises, we did improvisation exercises, and so on and so forth. And by the end of that, everybody was loose in one another's company." And it worked! The two weeks were invaluable for the cast, both new and old. Robert often paired with Rupert Grint, aka Ron Weasley, during the bonding camp and found Rupert just as funny in real life as his character. Robert said, "I didn't notice the transition to being accepted, but they are all really nice people. It seems like it should have been daunting but it wasn't."

That's not to say that everything was smooth sailing the whole time, though. Most of the maze scenes were scheduled to shoot in the early days of filming. Those scenes involved just him and Daniel Radcliffe, who plays Harry Potter. Daniel is a few years younger than Robert, and still had to spend five hours of every day in "school," working with a tutor on set. Rob had already finished with school (even the dreaded A levels). "I was just sitting by myself for ages," Robert said, "and at the time I wanted to be taken really seriously as an actor so I used to just sit around just drinking coffee all day and trying to look really intense." Looking intense probably wasn't too hard for Rob, not with those incredible eyes. . . .

The role of Cedric was physically demanding as well as mentally and emotionally challenging. Although Robert is an active young man (how else could he stay looking so fine?), being a Triwizard champion required more than simply being athletic. "It's a very physical part. The stuff in the maze, which was done in the beginning, was all on huge action sets," Robert told Virgin Media. "The hedges were huge and hydraulically operated. I got hit by stuff, getting pulled around by ropes, and Dan and I were running around punching each other so it was kind of vicious!"

Since the first two weeks of the shoot were just

Robert and Daniel in the maze—which was the final task of the Triwizard Tournament—he had to jump right into the most physical part of the shoot for him. Luckily he thoroughly enjoyed it! "The maze was really fun. A lot of the stunts are very contrived, and someone's practiced them a hundred times and you have to get it perfect otherwise it's pointless doing it. You're not gonna be in the right shot or anything. But in the maze, a lot of it was on Steadicam—which is just a guy running around with a camera." Sound too complicated and technical to picture clearly, even if you've seen the movie? Here's what it boils down to, in regular guy-speak: "Me and Dan were basically chasing each other around and punching each other, with these hedges squeezing us. And the camera would just follow you around, so you could basically do whatever you wanted. It was really fun. There were lots of cuts and bruises afterwards and it felt like you were doing a proper job!"

These male-bonding scenes continued to build on

the camaraderie that the cast had formed during their week of improvisation workshops. Robert felt confident in saying that those tournament filming scenes would have been a lot harder if it wasn't for director Mike Newell. He told one interviewer that it was the director who "came up with the idea that in the maze it is just the fear and the darkness and the isolation that kind of drives all the competitors a bit insane. We were really hyped up. You are on 100 percent adrenaline and you're starting this in the first week and you have just met all the other actors the week before and now you have to go crazy with them." The weeks of bonding before shooting allowed Robert and the other actors to reach a level of openness and connection necessary to produce such intense acting experiences.

Running and fighting weren't the only sports the actors had to excel in. They also had to master swimming on-screen, which is a lot trickier than simply swimming in a pool, as Robert is quick to tell anyone who asks. He spent approximately two months on the underwater scenes, which are a major part of the second task of the tournament. He had to take three weeks of scuba diving lessons before shooting those scenes. "There was a lot of underwater stuff which I quite liked, it got therapeutic after a while. I had never scuba dived before and the tank they taught us in was a little bathtub. The real thing was massive, like sixty feet deep and they expect you to just get in and act." Just imagine having to act without being able to breathe!

Even though he spent so much time learning the proper way to scuba dive, doing so in a bathtub-sized pool with lots of gear on and in a sixty-foot tank are like two different worlds. Robert had to swim underwater holding his breath, and then take "hits" of oxygen from divers in the tank with him. "On the first day of shooting in the tank, you have to hold your breath and there's nothing there!" Robert said. "There were a couple of times where you think you're swimming towards a guy with a breathing apparatus and then you find it's just some thing in the water," he said, and of course, not finding the oxygen made him freak out for a moment until he realized what to do. But alas, the cameras didn't stop rolling during that momentary panic. "They film your stupid face just screaming underwater, and then everyone starts laughing and it's just like, ahh, great!" Too bad those outtakes never made it to YouTube or the DVD extras, because Robert's "stupid face" is undoubtedly still completely heart melting. But it's a great example of Rob's good-natured spirit, which, along with his sense of humor, his ability to laugh at himself, and his willingness to throw himself so wholeheartedly into every single thing that he does, seems to make him stand out on every set, even in the everyday sort of moments.

Those key qualities are ones that many of the actors in *Goblet of Fire* shared, as working with action and special effects requires leaving dignity aside every once in a while. In an interview with *Disney Adventures* magazine, Robert mentioned how hard it was to dive heroically. "We had to do this scene looking like heroes diving into the lake. They had a stand-in doing perfect dives on the first take. Then Stan, Clémence, and I tried, but none of us could dive in right, and we all looked really stupid." Robert is sure the water scenes were the hardest part of filming *Goblet of Fire*, but in the end he found it quite calming. "You'd really concentrate on what you're supposed to be doing," he told a BBC interviewer. "You can't talk to anyone so you stay completely in character. You can't see anything so all you can hear is your director through the water, saying like 'look scared.' It was pretty fun. It was really fun!"

Keep in mind that this was Robert's first large film role. Though *Ring of the Nibelungs* included some special effects and action, a large-budget film like *Harry Potter and the Goblet of Fire* far outstrips what's possible on a made-for-television movie or even a film like *Vanity Fair*. "It was amazing. It was a very different thing to anything I've ever experienced," he said.

Nothing can compare to *Harry Potter*, especially for a modest young man who had just begun his film career. "The scale of Harry Potter is huge, people have been working on it for four or five years. There are two thousand people working on the set—not many films can afford that kind of 'epic-ness,'" he told Virgin Media.

Though it was like nothing Robert had done before, he wasn't about to let his amateur status or inexperience detract from his performance—even if he had to fib just a little to get the part in the first place. "I could barely swim before, but I told them in the audition that I could." Then again, who wouldn't tell a *tiny* little white lie in order to get a chance to break through like Robert did? And he might have gotten his comeuppance later, what with all those scuba-diving freak-outs caught on tape.

Just because Robert hadn't done much swimming before didn't mean he wasn't up to the challenge, and once he got the job, he made getting up to speed in that area a big priority. He quickly learned, though, that fitness drills aren't really his idea of fun. "I had to do a lot of fitness regimes and things in the beginning," he said in an interview with *Film Review* magazine. "I thought that would be pretty cool, because it would make me take it seriously. It was run by one of the stunt team, who are the most absurdly fit guys in the world. I can't even do ten press ups." For an active skier and snowboarder like Robert, the "regime" part of "fitness regime" wasn't the ideal exercise situation. "I did about three weeks of that, and in the end I think [the trainer] got so bored of trying to force me to do it that he wrote it all down so that I could do it at home." This worked out much better for both of them: Robert was able to keep in shape without getting bored, and his trainer didn't have to nag and pester him to do it. Most important of all, he was able to turn in a polished performance fighting his way through the maze with Daniel Radcliffe, swimming his way through the second task, and dealing with all of the other intensely physical moments of the Tri-wizard Tournament.

The less athletic scenes were sometimes a different story, though. The Yule Ball is the closest Hogwarts gets to having a prom, and it was a significant moment in the film. In one scene leading up to the ball, the stern Professor McGonagall teaches the students how to dance formally, and none of the guys are at all thrilled about learning this particular skill. Those weren't hard sentiments to act—the dancing scenes *were* a challenge. And since Robert never had a prom at his high school—there were only six students in his class!—he wasn't necessarily looking forward to this part of filming. "I think the Yule Ball is more attractive to the girls who read it," he said. "I never really thought 'Oh, I get to go to the ball!'" We can't expect even a hottie like Rob to be more excited by the scenes involving pretty gowns and dancing than the ones involving fear, fighting, and death around every corner, can we?

To properly prepare for the ballroom scene, all of the cast members involved in the Yule Ball had to take part in a choreography session that lasted two weeks. They learned the waltz, among other dances, and how to coordinate themselves while dancing as a large group, but only a few small bits of those lessons wound up being in the final cut of the movie. Even with all the dancing, "That was a really fun period," Robert told fans and reporters in a pre-movie press release with Katie Leung (Cho Chang) and Stanislav Ianevski (Viktor Krum). "Because I've never really done Renaissance . . . Is it Renaissance or a waltz? Some classical dancing. I really think I learned a lot."

Much to everyone's surprise, the classical dancing made them feel *less* self-conscious than the unchoreographed dancing scenes, like the dancing that happens to any fast song at a normal high school dance. Because "regular" dancing doesn't involve any standard moves, or strict choreography, Robert felt that it was harder—and it definitely made him more self-conscious—than waltzing. "I think the most embarrassing part of that was just the normal dancing. When the rock band comes. I think there was two days where the crew was like, 'Just dance, just dance.' That was really awkward," he told the press conference.

Robert also has the first major death scene in any of the Harry Potter movies. In the final Triwizard Tournament task, Harry and Cedric decide to share the prize, but instead of ending the tournament in glory, they are transported to a dark graveyard where the evil Lord Voldemort is waiting to return to his full power. Cedric is callously disposed of moments after their arrival in the graveyard with the killing curse Avada Kedavra, when Voldemort says to "Kill the spare." In 2008, *Entertainment Weekly* ranked this scene as number four in their "Twenty-five New Classic Death Scenes" list. They wrote, "Number Four: The murder of kind and decent Cedric Diggory. It's the darkest moment up to that point in the Potter saga, as

Harry experiences the death of someone close to him for the first time since he lost his parents. Meanwhile, he's forced to confront just how deadly his nemesis Voldemort is, and how likely it is that their clash may claim the lives of more innocents."

A good death scene can be something actors wait years to land, but Robert got his in his very first blockbuster role! Rather than agonizing over how dramatic or understated to play it, he took it all in stride, as any true professional would, and joked about the experience to reporters in between the rehearsals of the scene and its actual filming. "Well, I haven't actually died 'live' yet but I've been dead a few times. It's strange, but it's quite sort of relaxing. You feel like a bit of a therapist, because everyone's giving you all their grief, and you're just lying there listening. Yeah, it was quite nice, like no pressure after a couple weeks. I enjoyed it."

Though no day on a film set can truly be described as typical, Robert was kind enough to give fans a good idea of what shooting *Goblet of Fire* was like for him in the pre-release press conference with Katie and Stan. "There wasn't anything of any sort of structure," he said. "There would be days where hardly anything would happen, where you'd stand around the whole time because it was such a long shoot. Everything was shooting for about eleven months or something in total, so there were days and weeks where you would do absolutely nothing."

Generally Robert would have to be on set at six thirty in the morning. (Ack! That's too early!) In an interview on the *Goblet of Fire* DVD, Clémence Poésy (Fleur Delacour) said if actors arrived late to set, then they wouldn't have time to eat before they needed to be in hair and makeup. If Robert arrived at his usual six thirty, he'd be able to eat breakfast, then have his hair and makeup done, get into costume, and start work around nine. "Some days were just ridiculously busy while other days, especially when there is stunt work or something like that, [there was] a lot of time waiting around," he said in the press conference. Regardless of the early mornings and the unpredictable schedule, Robert would never complain about his time on the *Goblet of Fire* set. When the BBC asked him if there were any "bad parts" about shooting the film, Robert's answer was an unequivocal "No!" He said, "It was a really long shoot so it was kinda tiring by the end, but all in all it was really fun, and there were a lot of amazing periods, which was really nice."

5
More than
Just a Pretty Face

"He's a beautiful musician, a very creative soul, very similar to Edward."
—Catherine Hardwicke

Edward Cullen is the quintessential hot hero to Twi-lighters around the world, but who is Robert Pattinson's hero? Well, Robert has said he'd love to play Gambit from *X-Men*. And when the *Los Angeles Times* asked him which superhero he'd like to play, he claimed Spider-Man would be cool—for a slightly surprising reason: "I like the outfit; I like a little bit of spandex." And who wouldn't like to see Robert *in* a little spandex? Hopefully studio heads are taking note and picturing

Robert as the next big comic book superhero on the docket, because his fans certainly now are!

In all seriousness, Robert admires many of the great actors in the generations before him. For the role of Edward, he drew on a number of iconic performances. "There are bits of *Rebel Without a Cause* and stuff," he said to joblo.com, referring to the great young movie star of the fifties, James Dean. Performances such as Dean's helped him get an initial handle on a character who is very much a loner and endlessly complex. Edward is Robert's first film role with an American accent. Luckily he didn't find it to be too much of a challenge. When MTV asked how he went about learning to mimic one, he said, "I grew up watching American movies and stuff, so I've learned how to 'act' from American films." There's not necessarily a particular actor that he modeled the accent after, though, unless it was by accident. "At the beginning, when I was doing the first couple scenes, I kept slipping into different actors," he said. Then he laughed, and added, "During a really dramatic scene, you start doing Al Pacino."

As far as vampire inspiration goes, Robert names Gary Oldman as one of his favorite movie vampires. Oldman played Count Dracula in the 1992 movie adaptation of Bram Stoker's novel *Dracula*. "I also like the actor in the original *Nosferatu*. He's amazing. I mean, he has an amazing face. I thought he was really cool," he continued. *Nosferatu* is a very old silent film. Made in Germany in 1922, before movies had sound, it starred Max Schreck as the villainous vampire. Clearly, when Robert decides to research roles, he takes it seriously! To him, taking in the classics of the vampire movie genre is just as essential as reading the entire Twilight Saga in order to fully formulate and "become" his idea of Edward.

The actor that Robert most admires has never played a vampire—Jack Nicholson. He admits that as a young teen, he felt a bit of hero worship for the legendary actor. He said in an interview, "I aspire to be

Jack Nicholson. I love every single mannerism. I used to try and be him in virtually everything I did, I don't know why. I watched *One Flew Over the Cuckoo's Nest* when I was about thirteen, and I dressed like him. I tried to do his accent. I did everything like him. I think it's kind of stuck with me." Jack Nicholson is one of the most acclaimed actors in American film, with a broad range of roles in his repertoire, and he has collected awards for a variety of nuanced and subtle roles, as well as more over-the-top ones. So a career like his is definitely a worthy aspiration for a young actor shooting to fame.

In the same way, Robert has made varied choices that have led to not only blockbuster, much-hyped roles, such as Cedric Diggory and Edward Cullen, but also roles in independent films like *How to Be* and *Little Ashes*, so his dream of being like Jack Nicholson is on track so far.

Jack Nicholson is even the inspiration for Robert's stage name as a musician: Bobby Dupea. Bobby Dupea is the main character (played by Nicholson, of course) in the 1970 movie *Five Easy Pieces*. In the movie, Bobby is a gifted concert pianist who comes from a well-off family of musicians. But he is a restless and sometimes angry young man; so to escape the dull, sheltered routine of practice and performance, he takes off on the road to see the world. Eventually, though, he does reunite with his family, having experienced many important moments that allowed him to come to know himself as a more well-rounded human being. So why is this the name that Rob chose as his "incognito" cover as a musician? Well, there's the obvious Robert-Bobby link, and there's a clear tip of the hat to Jack Nicholson, too. Perhaps Robert even sometimes dreams of running away from his ever-growing fame to "see the world." But the deepest reason of all may be one that *Seventeen* magazine got him to admit . . . that his dream job is being a pianist—just like Bobby Dupea in *Five Easy Pieces*!

Music has been a large part of Robert's world from

a very young age, partly because of his sister's success. He's seen that it takes a lot of work and dedication, but that it's actually a career in which it's possible to have great success. Having watched his sister's interests develop, the tremendously creative Robert had to try his hand at music, too. Just as *Goblet of Fire* was hitting the screens around the world, he told *Movie Magic*, "I have been playing the piano for my entire life—since I was three or four. And the guitar—I used to play classical guitar from when I was about five to twelve years of age. Then I didn't play guitar for like years. About four or five years ago, I got out the guitar again and just started playing blues and stuff. I am not very good at the guitar, but I am all right. I am in a band in London as well." That band was called Bad Girls, and was started by his first girlfriend's then-current boyfriend. How's that for awkward! Perhaps it's not surprising that Robert is no longer with that band.

The band he's with now is unnamed, or at least he

wouldn't admit its name to a persistent fan who asked about it during a signing at a convention. But he did say that they play gigs in London and did a festival in Wales. So who knows? Maybe one day if you're in London, you'll run into Robert and his mates jamming out in the most unexpected of spots!

What legendary musicians does Robert love? Who is his Jack Nicholson equivalent in the music world? Funnily enough, when Robert was in junior high, his musical heroes were Eminem and Jay Kay from Jamiroquai, since he was "really into rap" at that time, he told the BBC. These days, his music is much more low-key. He likes blues and country-inspired rock. His sound is folksy and almost Bob Dylan–like—he, too, can play the guitar and the harmonica at the same time.

Could a career in music lure Robert away from acting entirely? It's possible, but if so, then landing the role as Edward may have recharged both his acting career *and*—unexpectedly—his musical aspirations.

In the novel, Edward is a gifted pianist. (Are we sensing a theme?) After all, it's not like he has a whole lot to do during long nights, since vampires in Stephenie Meyer's universe don't need sleep. *Twilight* is chock-full of achingly romantic scenes between Bella and Edward, but the most heart-melting scene of all may be when Edward sits down at the beautiful grand piano in his home and plays the song he has composed for Bella. What does this song sound like? It's the question that Twihards everywhere are dying to know the answer to. And since Robert was cast as Edward and the great "Is he hot enough?" debate was laid to rest—at least by most—it may be the next biggest question that fans have devoted themselves to pondering.

Everyone has an idea of what the song *should* sound like, and fans have been unafraid to lobby their selections to Stephenie and the *Twilight* director, Catherine Hardwicke. Many suspected it would be a reinterpretation of one of the songs on Stephenie's

Twilight-inspired list, or maybe even an original composition by her favorite band, Muse. When he signed on for the part, musical ability wasn't on the checklist of necessary attributes, so no one involved in the movie anticipated that Robert himself might pen the all-important song. That he ended up doing so was a dream come true, both for the moviemakers and the waiting fans! But that's exactly what happened, and now it seems the most obvious possibility of all.

After all, Robert had kept up with his music while on the *Twilight* set. Like most musicians, his music is deeply rooted, a part of his soul, and a key to his creative process. And like any passionate person, he is driven to do the things that feed him creatively, and for Rob, that thing is making music. So it's not something Rob could just quit doing during the months of filming. It's not at all surprising, then, that he found ways to satisfy his musical urges while on set, filling up off-set moments and allowing him to diffuse some of the stresses of playing the intense character of Edward. "I was doing music before I started acting," Robert said, "so I still have bits and pieces, and I've been playing in Portland [during the shoot]." But his music playing and writing couldn't be contained by impromptu offstage performances. He revealed to MTV, "The lullaby thing, I just made [it] up on the spot during the scene. During the scene, I drifted into the piano playing. I guess it just comes from somewhere." And director Catherine Hardwicke, a wildly creative and artistic soul herself, recognizes genius when she sees it.

Catherine cast Robert as Edward in the first place, knowing that no one else would be as perfect in the role, and it's clear that she's as delighted with his musical ability as with his acting ability. "He's a beautiful musician, a very creative soul, very similar to Edward. He just totally reads the most interesting stuff, and sees the most interesting movies, and is very introspective and diving into his existential self," she said. So when it came time for "Bella's Lullaby" to be created, she gave him free rein to see what he could do. "I told him he should write one, and let's see if we can make it work, because that would be really cool if it was Rob's song." Cool? That may be the biggest understatement of the century!

Catherine couldn't confirm that Robert's impromptu "Bella's Lullaby" made the final cut. She said to MTV, "'Bella's Lullaby,' actually . . . that's a beautiful love theme that develops and goes all the way through the movie. You see it like in the most beginning parts, and then it gets really into the full song in the middle [of the movie], and then you hear bits of it later. But Rob has two other songs in the movie." When prodded to reveal more about Robert's compositions prior to the movie's release, Catherine demurred, wanting fans to experience it for themselves when they see the movie. What she did reveal was that "they're really beautiful love songs, like heartbreaking. I cried the first time I heard the two songs. They're deep; they're very soulful." Kristen Stewart, the actress who plays

Bella, agrees and confirms Catherine's faith in Robert's music, saying simply, "He plays spontaneously, brilliantly."

Stephenie Meyer never expected the movie casting directors to find a guy who looked so much like the Edward in her mind, so she was doubly delighted that Robert not only looked perfect but was a musician, too. In an early MTV interview about the making of the movie, she was happily surprised by that revelation. "That's something I didn't know," she said. "I've never heard him play, so it's kind of hard to say [whether his lullaby will be as I imagined it]. If it worked out right, it would be really cool." Music has been indispensable to Stephenie's writing process from the start, and for all four books. She explained to the *Los Angeles Times*, "The music is a part of (my writing process). I could not do without it." She elaborated on that process to *Rolling Stone*, saying, "I listen to music always when I write. When I hear music on the radio, I'm like 'Oh! That's a song for this character' or 'This one would so fit that character in this mood!'"

Stephenie's tastes in music are maybe a bit more edgy than Robert's folksy style, though, since she leans toward alternative and progressive metal. Her favorite band *is* British, a trio called Muse, whose song "Time Is Running Out" is part of Stephenie's personal *Twilight* playlist, along with music from bands like Linkin Park and My Chemical Romance. So it's no surprise that Muse is an official part of the movie soundtrack—or that Stephenie's passion for the band was also shared by the moviemakers. Another favorite band of hers, Blue October, fronted by Justin Furstenfeld, played a number of concerts coinciding with the release of *Breaking Dawn*. Stephenie discovered Blue October when she heard the single "Hate Me" in the car one day. She said to *Rolling Stone* that it sounded "like Edward was singing out of my radio."

Though Robert may differ from Stephenie on favorite styles of music, it's obvious that they share a passion for it, and that fact will only serve their collaboration well. Fans in the United Kingdom may be lucky enough to hear some of Robert's musical work in the gigs he and his band play around London, but U.S. fans will have to settle for hearing him perform in *Twilight*. Though Robert did have a MySpace music page under his stage name, Bobby Dupea, he's made the profile private and gone incognito for the time being. Music is still a very personal facet of his life, and he probably isn't quite ready for the multitudes of fans to discover it. For now, anyway. It doesn't seem like too much to hope that with his well-earned time off, he'll finally get around to making the album he's wanted to record for years—and maybe even go on an American tour!

The *Twilight* Phenomenon

"There's something that happens to you when you're first introduced to the phenomenon that is *Twilight*... it ignites something inside of you." —*H Magazine*

In 2003, around the same time that Robert Pattinson first met *Goblet of Fire* director Mike Newell, a woman named Stephenie Meyer had a dream. Back then, no one particularly cared what Stephenie Meyer dreamed, or thought, or even wrote, because Stephenie Meyer wasn't a name anyone knew yet—she was a wife and mom living in Arizona. Shocking as it seems now, when there's a world full of extremely loyal and vocal fans who can think of little else, back then, Edward

Cullen, Bella Swan, and Jacob Black existed in only one person's imagination.

Four years later, *Twilight* has sold ten million copies and counting, but as the bestselling author tells it, the novel started on June 2, 2003, with that single dream. Stephenie's dream was about first love, in the most intense possible way. Eventually that dream was transformed into the famous "meadow scene" in the book, in which Bella first sees Edward in his full glittering, vampiric glory, and they profess their love for each other, all the while knowing it could mean a tragic end. This swoon-worthy moment was one of the most anticipated movie scenes for fans, who hoped that Robert Pattinson and Kristen Stewart's chemistry would match the power of the scene they have imagined in their own minds, as they read (and reread) the novel. Luckily Stephenie has a well-trafficked website where she could assure her Twilighters that it would. After a visit to the set, she crowed that *Twilight* devotees were going to get all they hoped for and more. Gleeful, she wrote, "They are amazing actors. . . . They are channeling Edward and Bella like nobody's business."

Let's get back to that spicy dream. How—*exactly*—did that climactic moment between Edward and Bella begin? We can all be thankful that Stephenie woke with it still in her mind in such vivid detail. As she remembers it, a strikingly beautiful vampire boy and an ordinary teenage girl stood in a sunny meadow, talking about their extraordinary connection. Something was compelling them to be together . . . and yet how could that be? They were doomed because of one unavoidable truth: Every second they were together, the vampire was longing to kill the girl. And then Stephenie woke up.

Like anyone waking up in the middle of a great dream before she wanted to, Stephenie was *Not. Pleased. At. All.* She wanted to know more, to keep eavesdropping on this fascinating and beautiful couple—and she couldn't stop thinking about what might have happened for the star-crossed teens. She ended up not mentioning it to her husband, and she knew that she couldn't just call her friends or siblings and tell them about the dream. As she later said to CBS News, "Everybody *hates* that!" Still, she continued to wonder—constantly—about what might happen next for the oddly matched couple in her dream.

So in between the tasks of her day—making lunch, taking her three small sons, then ages one, three, and five, to swimming lessons—Stephenie decided to try capturing the dream on paper. She began to write the rest of the scene as she imagined it, conjuring as much of the moody atmosphere as she could. She wrote ten pages that day, but felt like she wasn't typing fast enough to keep up with what was happening as the story unfolded inside her head. Somehow, she'd managed to tap back into the force that had created the dream in the first place, but harnessing it was another matter. So she wrote again the next day, and the next, and soon she had moved a desk into the middle of her living room so that she could write while watching her children play.

Stephenie had earned her English degree from Brigham Young University in 1995, so she was no stranger to writing. But this was unlike any writing experience she'd ever had before. The story positively flowed from her fingertips, in a way that her college English papers had never seemed to do. Stephenie could hear the couple's voices clearly in her head. All she had to do was keep up with their conversations. She got the bulk of her writing done late at night, while her family slept, music blasting through her headphones—music that she would soon come to think of as the soundtrack for her story. She realized that music was an integral part of story writing for her. In the years since *Twilight*'s publication, Stephenie has published playlists for each of the four books in the Twilight Saga on her website, explaining to fans that the songs inspired her while writing. Sometimes they have even suggested plotlines or character development. As she explained to *Rolling Stone*, several years after the totally unexpected first blaze of writing that became *Twilight*, and even after the books had become an explosive success, "I really don't think you get a dream like that more than once in your lifetime. And I didn't need it; once I had the story and it unlocked the writer inside me, I had enough ideas on my own."

As she wrote, Stephenie got up the courage to tell her older sister, Emily, about the book and eventually let her read along, chapter by chapter, as it flowed out of her. Emily is an avid *Buffy the Vampire Slayer* fan, so of course she suggested that Stephenie borrow the *Buffy* DVDs to see another take on how the vampire myths and legends could exist in a modern high school setting. But Stephenie was adamant about not wanting other influences in her head as she wrote. Interviewers are often shocked to discover that for an author of vampire stories, Stephenie is surprisingly unfamiliar with the canon of vampire books and movies. Fans of the Twilight Saga should be relieved that Stephenie played the role of stubborn little sister and *didn't* listen to Emily's advice. The end result was that Stephenie created the original world of *Twilight* and its dazzlingly different vampire citizens all from her own vivid imagination.

Stephenie's vampires aren't your typical vampires. They're vampire "vegetarians"—they don't allow themselves to enjoy human prey. They abstain from drinking human blood, and instead they hunt animals, from mountain lions to elk to grizzlies, and drink *their* blood. As Stephenie explains to fans on her MySpace profile, "It's like living on a diet forever, no cheating. Sigh." A hard limitation to set on yourself, but it's a sacrifice that her vampires—the good ones, at least—have decided they are willing to make.

With the Cullen family—the coven of vampires who are the pseudo-family to which Edward belongs—Stephenie was proud that she'd invented a whole new kind of mythology for the vampires that lived in her world. These were not vampires who could only come out at night, or ones who were hunted down with crosses and garlic. Not at all! Her vampires are, essentially, made from living stone. They are incredibly strong, amazingly fast, and perfectly gorgeous creatures. They stay out of the sun not because it burns them, but because they have a tendency to sparkle in it. The stonelike substance that makes up their bodies holds facets of light, just like diamonds. Basically they are enhanced in every way possible from the humans they once were before becoming vampires. Oh, and they can only be killed by being torn apart from limb to limb, and then burned (easy, right?). All of these details, and their accuracy within the *Twilight* universe, matter enormously to Stephenie and her fans. That's why much later, when it came time to sell movie rights, Stephenie had to go to someone who would honor what she had created and her fans loved. It was director Catherine Hardwicke's similar vision—that and her promise of "No garlic, no crosses, no fangs!"—that won Stephenie's trust that she was giving her imagined world to the right person, the one who could bring it to cinematic life.

Stephenie *was* thinking about a movie, even as she wrote the first draft of *Twilight*. Not that she believed the book would even get published when she was first starting—*that* would have been crazy, a chance in a zillion! But it was *fun* casting the actors in her head. She explained to fans later on premiere.com, "I saw the book very visually as I was writing it," so picturing a movie was a natural extension. "Just to see one scene of it on the big screen [would be worth it]," she went on. "I didn't care about anyone else going to see it. This was about me, alone, in the theater getting to see it on the screen and having it be real, and that's what swayed me [to take the risk allowing it to become Catherine Hardwicke's movie]."

But let's get back to how *Twilight* ever got into the hands of its very first fan to begin with. Stephenie had that pivotal dream at the beginning of June, and by the end of August, she had a completed novel manuscript in her hands. That's none too shabby for the equivalent of a summer vacation! Once she had that finished piece of writing, she began to send the manuscript out to literary agents, with the stand-in title, *Forks,* after the town in Washington State that serves as the setting for much of the story's action. It was then that things started to happen for Stephenie, and happen with a speed that first-time authors rarely experience. But then again, she had already known that this story wasn't like any other. She crossed her fingers, hoping that other people would recognize that, too.

Inevitably, they did. Jodi Reamer, an agent with Writers House, a highly regarded New York literary agency, called soon after reading the manuscript, asking to represent Stephenie and her novel. In one of the first significant decisions about the book, before sending the manuscript out to editors, Jodi suggested that she and Stephenie try to find a new title "with more atmosphere." They brainstormed for a week, and the result was *Twilight*—evocative, sweeping, lush, and now familiar to millions of readers. Interestingly enough, though, there simply may not be a perfect title for this book, Stephenie says on her website. When the book began to be published in different countries, hardly any stuck with the title *Twilight*. In Germany, the book is called *Until Dawn*, but in German it sounds like *until bite*, so the German title is a vampire pun. In Finland, the title is *Temptation*, and in France, *Fascination*. The Japanese publisher split *Twilight* into three separate books: *The Boy I Love Is a Vampire, Blood Tastes Sadness,* and *The Vampire Family in the Darkness.*

Once Stephenie had the perfect title (at least for America), off the manuscript went to publishing houses. Then, with vampirelike speed, Stephenie had an editor. Megan Tingley, of Little, Brown Books for Young Readers, was so taken by Stephenie's vision that she decided she wanted to publish not just *Twilight*, but two more books, which Stephenie hadn't even written yet.

Twilight was published on October 5, 2005, and almost instantly, readers embraced it. Why? Well, for a million reasons, many of them Edward, Edward, and . . . Edward! But one of the other reasons is the very one that Robert Pattinson himself mentioned to MTV: "It's very intimate. . . . At the core of *Twilight*, it's a love story. It's a very intense love story, which differentiates it. Everything else just goes away."

Not only did readers embrace and love the book, they wanted to *talk* about it. They wanted to talk about Bella, about Edward, about romance, and choices, and the perfect guy, and all the oh-so-sexy moments between these characters that feel incredibly *real*. So *Twilight* fans flocked to the Internet. Many of them had done the same a few years earlier, when they read and loved the Harry Potter books and wanted to find other people who did, too. Within a month of *Twilight*'s release, fan sites began popping up. And those early fan sites were lucky beyond their wildest dreams—they often got drop-in visits from Stephenie Meyer herself. Stephenie was just as eager to talk to her readers as they were to talk to her. She read their fan fiction, answered questions about the mythology of her vampire world, and was genuinely awed by the fervor of the teens who loved her story. Stephenie had never actually heard of MySpace before she began visiting *Twilight* fan sites, but once the Twihards told her about it, she signed up. Today she has more than 75,000 MySpace friends! Her Top 25 includes her absolute favorite band, Muse; actor Henry Cavill, who Stephenie once hoped would play the role of Edward; her publicist, Elizabeth; and her younger brother, Jacob (!), to name a few. She also helped establish some of the fan sites in those early days. She supported Lori Joffs, a Nashville stay-at-home mom who founded The Twilight Lexicon (www.twilightlexicon. com), by providing backstories and other intriguing details about the characters and the world of *Twilight* that couldn't be found anywhere else at the time.

For the next three years, each end of summer meant not just that school was about to start, but that Stephenie had published a new addition to what became known as the Twilight Saga. As each one hit the bookstores, the clamor and love for the books grew and grew, with markers such as the *New York Times* bestsellerdom for every volume, thousands upon thousands of book preorders by eager fans, and sold-out "Twilight Proms." Some of the proms had the luck to host Stephenie herself, like the five-hundred-guest sold-out event on May 5, 2007, at Arizona State University, where Stephenie got into the prom spirit herself, arriving in a gorgeous burgundy gown with her dark hair curled in ringlets.

Twilight had become a phenomenon! With that came growing anticipation about the issue at the heart of the stories: Who would Bella Swan choose to devote herself to? Would it be her faithful but absent vampire love, Edward? Or dependable, lovable Jacob Black, the werewolf who is always there when she needs him? Before long, readers began proclaiming their loyalty for one suitor over the other in public places, wearing customized shirts—and even shoes!—emblazoned with the words TEAM JACOB or TEAM EDWARD. They started even more fan sites, along with MySpace and Facebook groups to discuss the many reasons why they felt that Bella would eventually see things their way.

Most of all, though, readers simply talked about the books. They gulped down each new book, usually in one frenzied night of must-know-the-ending reading, and then passed it to their friends, sisters, cousins, and boyfriends. Obviously some girls have better luck than others in getting their boyfriends to read it. But it's not just people their own ages that *Twilight* fans share the book with. They also share it with their moms, who have become just as besotted as their daughters. In fact, one of the most active online fan sites is called Twilight Moms (www.twilightmoms.com), which labels itself a home for fans of Stephenie Meyer